EXPLORERS, TRAPPERS, AND PIONEERS

Ellen H. Todras

KINGFISHER

NEW YORK

All About America: EXPLORERS, TRAPPERS, AND PIONEERS

KINGFISHER
LONDON & NEW YORK

The All About America series was produced for Kingfisher by Bender Richardson White, Uxbridge, U.K.
Editor: Lionel Bender
Designer: Ben White
DTP: Neil Sutton
Production: Kim Richardson
Consultant: Richard Jensen, Research Professor of History, Culver Stockton College, Missouri

Sources of quotations and excerpts
page 4, Norsemen: Bishop, Morris, and Norman Kotker. *The Horizon Book of the Middle Ages*. NY: American Heritage, 1968, page 28.
pages 5, 7, 14: Morris, Richard B., and the editors of Time-Life Books. *The New World*. NY: Time-Life Books, 1963, pages 11, 32, 37.
pages 8, 12: Hale, John R., and the editors of Time-Life Books. *Age of Exploration*. Alexandria, VA: Time-Life Books, 1974, pages 105, 139.
page 8, sidebar: http://www.mexconnect.com/articles/1538-the-spanish-conquest-1519-1521
page 15: "Jamestown," www.britannica.com
page 19: http://gocalifornia.about.com/cs/missioncalifornia/a/fr_serra.htm?p=1
pages 21, 22: Andrist, Ralph K., and the editors of *American Heritage. To the Pacific with Lewis and Clark*. NY: American Heritage, 1967, pages 43, 60, 93.
page 24: Gilbert, Bill, and the editors of Time-Life Books. *The Trailblazers*. NY: Time-Life Books, 1973, page 47.
page 29: Horn, Huston, and the editors of Time-Life Books. *The Pioneers*. NY: Time-Life Books, 1974, pages 192, 193.
page 29, sidebar: http://www.library.cornell.edu/Reps/DOCS/landrush.htm [William Willard Howard in *Harper's Weekly* 33 (May 18, 1889), pages 391–394].

Acknowledgments
The publishers would like to thank the following illustrators for their contribution to this book: Mark Bergin, Peter Dennis, Adam Hook, John James, James Field, Mike White, Gerald Wood, and Paul Wright. Map: Neil Sutton.
Book cover design: Neal Cobourne.
Cover artwork: Mike White.
The publishers thank the following for supplying photos for this book: b = bottom, c = center, l = left, t = top, m = middle: © The Bridgeman Art Library: pages 10–11c (© Czartoryski Museum, Kraków, Poland); 13tl (National Maritime Museum, London, U.K.); 14–15bc (© Wallace Collection, London, U.K.); 17tl • © Getty Images: pages 20–21c (Nativestock.com/Marilyn Angel Wynn); 22–23bc (Ira Block) • The Granger Collection/TopFoto: cover, pages 1c; 4tl; 5t; 6tl; 6–7c; 7tr; 7br; 8m; 8bl; 8–9c; 9bl; 9tr; 10m; 11br; 12–13c; 12c; 13m; 13mr; 14–15tc; 15tr; 16m; 17m; 18tl; 18b; 19t; 20m; 20b; 21tr; 23b; 24tl; 24br; 26–27bc; 27b; 28–29c; 29ml; 29b • © istockphoto.com: pages 12tl (scol22); 26m (Scuddy Waggoner) • © Library of Congress: pages 1, 2–3, 30–31, 32 (pnp/ppmsca.23728); 26tl (pnp/cph.3g03941); 26bl (pnp/ppmsca.23728); 26br (pnp/ppmsca.03143); 28 (pnp/ppmsc.02536)
Every effort has been made to trace the copyright holders of the images. The publishers apologize for any omissions.

Note to readers: The website addresses listed in this book are correct at the time of publishing. However, due to the ever-changing nature of the Internet, website addresses and content can change. Websites can contain links that are unsuitable for children. The publisher cannot be held responsible for changes in website addresses or content or for information obtained through third-party websites. We strongly advise that Internet searches should be supervised by an adult.

CONTENTS

Introduction

Explorers, Trappers, and Pioneers looks at the exploration and settlement of North America from earliest recorded times to the year 1890. It highlights the journeys of European explorers who were looking for a new ocean route to Asia. Instead they found America, calling it the New World. Other explorers and colonists traveled inland and started to build homes. Some settlers traded furs and other goods with American Indians. Pioneers ventured into unknown territories, surveyed the land, and helped set up trails and, later, railroads. By 1890, settlers had reached all parts of the nation. The story is presented as a series of double-page articles, each one looking at a particular topic. It is illustrated with paintings, engravings, and photographs from the time mixed with artists' impressions of everyday scenes and situations.

Crossing the Atlantic
The earliest travelers to North America

More than 1,000 years ago, tall, warlike people from Scandinavia in northern Europe set sail to the west. They were Vikings, and they became the first Europeans to settle in North America.

In the A.D. 700s and 800s, the Vikings sailed to England and France in order to raid towns and farms. They killed anyone who opposed them. Europeans were so scared of the Vikings, whom they called the Norsemen or Northmen, that they made a prayer about them: "From the fury of the Northmen, deliver us, O Lord!"

Vinland

▶ The Vikings named Newfoundland Vinland—*vin* is an old European word for meadow. This is believed to be an early Viking map of their known world.

▲ A finely carved Viking ship's figurehead

Island-Hopping Vikings

Not long after the Vikings were named Northmen, they became Christians and grew more civilized. They used boats called knorrs for long-distance travel. The wide belly of the knorrs provided room for passengers and cargo. These superb sailors settled Iceland beginning in about 900. One Icelandic settler, Eric the Red, fled Iceland in his boat after killing another settler. He founded a settlement in Greenland in 982. From Greenland, Viking explorers continued their westward migration. In 1000, they sailed to the coast of Newfoundland, in eastern Canada.

Map labels: Greenland; North America; Columbia River; Fort Mandan; Missouri River; Fort Dubois; St. Louis; Cape Cod; Mississippi River; Gulf of Mexico; Pacific Ocean; Atlantic Ocean; N

Vikings' route
Lewis & Clark's route
Columbus's route

Exploring North America

The first European explorers mapped the eastern coast and then made their way inland along big rivers. The West was explored from the Pacific Ocean and Central America long before routes across the country were set up.

Landing on the American coast

Much of what we know about the Vikings in Vinland comes from Norse sagas—old stories that told about heroes and their deeds. The sagas tell of the good farmland in Vinland. They also tell about meetings with the native people, whom the Vikings called Skrellings and who were hostile to the Norse settlers. After a few years, the Vikings abandoned the settlement rather than live a "life of constant dread and turmoil."

Evidence for Vinland

Until recently, people questioned the truth of the Viking sagas about Vinland. In 1960, however, a fisherman in Newfoundland found some sod formations of homes that had been abandoned long ago. They were shaped like old Scandinavian houses. Archaeologists visited and uncovered Viking objects and artifacts dated to A.D. 1000. So there is truth in the sagas. Nearly 500 years passed before another European traveled to North America.

▲ This woodcut shows a Viking fighting with an Inuit of Greenland. The landmark of Hvitserkr means "high mountain."

Greenland

Located in the North Atlantic Ocean, Greenland is the largest island in the world. The Vikings dominated the native Inuit population. Greenland's Norse settlements declined in the 1400s and no longer existed by the 1500s.

▼ The Vikings had immense skill and courage to sail the distances that they did. They kept close to shore when possible and navigated by reading the currents and the stars.

A Short-Lived Settlement

Experts think that the Viking men and women who settled in Vinland stayed for only a few years. There are no burial grounds there, and no stables or barns for animals have been found.

Columbus Arrives
The earliest explorers to America

Christopher Columbus led one of the most famous explorations of all time, and his journey led to one of the biggest surprises ever: the discovery of the Americas. This discovery marked the beginning of a new era in history.

In the 1400s, Europeans sailed east around the tip of Africa to get to Asia. One Italian, Christopher Columbus, had an unusual idea about reaching Asia: he thought of sailing west, across the Atlantic Ocean. Columbus convinced King Ferdinand and Queen Isabella of Spain to finance this voyage. He left Spain in 1492, with a fleet of three ships. The crew had never before sailed for so long without reaching land. On October 10, they wanted to turn back. Columbus kept two journals of the trip—one for himself, with accurate distances, and one that he shared with the crew, with underestimated distances. He persuaded them to continue westward. On October 12, 1492, the lookout cried, "Land! Land!"

▲ Columbus was made a nobleman in Spain and got a coat of arms because of his voyage. The lower left portion of the coat of arms represents the islands he discovered.

◀ Two of the three ships on Columbus's first voyage that sailed into the unknown

▼ Christopher Columbus steps ashore to meet the Taíno (Arawak) Indians, who were friendly at first but who grew to distrust the Europeans.

A New World

Like many Europeans of his time, Christopher Columbus viewed people of cultures different from his own as savages. When he met the Taíno (Arawak) Indians on San Salvador, he called them Indians, thinking he was near India. Over the next century, many American Indians died, either from diseases brought by Europeans or from being enslaved.

Not the place he meant to be!

Columbus landed on an island in the Caribbean Sea and named it San Salvador. Then he traveled to other Caribbean islands, sure that he had found islands off the coast of China. He left 40 crew members on the island of Hispaniola to look for gold. He brought parrots, spices, gold, and human captives back to Spain. Thrilled with Columbus's supposed achievement, Ferdinand and Isabella rewarded him.

Columbus made three more sea voyages to the Americas. In one, he in fact landed on the northern coast of South America. He never recognized his great discovery, continuing to seek evidence of Asia. Yet he started a chain of events that modern America can trace as its origins.

◄ A bronze astrolabe used by Portuguese sailors in the 1500s

Beyond Columbus's First Steps

England and France joined Spain in the race to explore and claim land in the Americas. In 1497, John Cabot explored the eastern coast of Canada for England. In 1502, Amerigo Vespucci explored the South American coastline for Spain. A mapmaker called the Americas the "land of Americus, for Americus its discoverer," and the name stuck. In 1513, the Spanish explorer Vasco Núñez de Balboa became the first European to see the Pacific Ocean from present-day Panama on its western shore.

◄ The astrolabe was an instrument that allowed explorers to calculate the height of the sun. From that, they could figure out their latitude—how far north or south they were. There was no instrument to calculate longitude—how far east or west—until the mid-1700s.

The Conquistadors
Exploration and plunder

The conquistadors were the Spanish soldiers and explorers of the early 1500s who conquered Mexico, Central America, and Peru. They were the advance guard, planting a Spanish empire in the Americas.

Conquistador Hernando Cortés once said, "We Spaniards suffer from a disease that only gold can cure." Cortés determined to conquer the Aztecs of Mexico to fulfill his appetite for gold. He landed on Mexico's eastern coast in 1519, with about 500 soldiers. The ruler of the Aztecs sent treasures to keep Cortés out of the capital city, Tenochtitlán. But these gifts made Cortés want more. He invaded Tenochtitlán, helped by Indians who were the Aztecs' enemies. In 1521, Cortés destroyed the city and began to build Mexico City on its foundations.

▲ A conquistador hacks through thick jungle growth with his sword.

▲ The gold used for this medal of King Philip II of Spain came from the Americas.

▼ In the spring of 1519, Hernando Cortés and a small army landed at Veracruz. The conquest of Mexico left the local civilizations in ruins.

Guns, Horses, and Swords
The technology of European conquest was unknown to the Aztecs. They thought Cortés's ships were "towers floating on the sea." They had never seen horses before and thought men riding horses were "man-beasts." And the Aztec arrows were no match for the Spanish guns and swords.

◄ Hernando Cortés (1485–1547), Spanish conqueror of Mexico

Spanish Wealth

The wealth of gold and silver from Mexico and Peru changed life in Spain. Because there was so much more money, prices doubled. Spanish wealth spread throughout Europe like ripples in a pond. It led to a rise of trade and commerce and a greater gap between the rich and poor.

▼ Pizarro made the Inca ruler Atahuallpa his captive. Inca citizens brought gold objects to Pizarro for Atahuallpa's ransom.

▼ An explorer's painting of an Aztec woman grinding cacao tree beans to make chocolate

Crops, Cacao, and Disease

European exploration of the Americas changed the world in ways the conquistadors never imagined. They introduced exotic foods into the European diet: the potato, the tomato, squash, corn, beans, and cacao (from which comes chocolate). Explorers also found the Indian hammock a sensible way to sleep, especially on ships. But the diseases the explorers carried and passed on, such as smallpox, killed thousands of Indians, who had no immunity to them.

A room stuffed with gold

In 1532, another Spaniard, Francisco Pizarro, reached Peru with a small army of 62 horsemen and 102 foot soldiers. The king of the Inca Empire in Peru, Atahuallpa, met Pizarro in the town of Cajamarca. Hordes of Incas accompanied Atahuallpa, many unarmed. Atahuallpa believed that he had nothing to fear from Pizarro's army.

A Spanish priest asked Atahuallpa to accept the Christian God. When Atahuallpa refused, the priest ordered an attack. The Spanish fired into the crowds, and Atahuallpa was taken prisoner. He offered to fill a room with gold and silver in exchange for his freedom. Pizarro agreed but did not stick to his agreement. He had Atahuallpa killed. By 1533, the mighty Inca Empire had come to a sudden end.

◄ A gold pendant from Mexico of the Mixtec god of the dead. It was made around 1400.

Exploring the Coast
Spain and France battle for settlements

The conquistadors were eager to explore the land north of Mexico and claim it for Spain. French explorers were equally eager to claim the land for their country. Conflicts flared from this contest of nations.

▲ The settlers at the French colony of Charlesfort struggled to survive. They failed at growing crops and were rescued by English ships.

In the early 1500s, the Spanish conquistador Juan Ponce de León explored the Caribbean. Indians told him about an island with a fountain of youth. In search of this, Ponce de León sailed farther west. In 1513, he landed on the coast near modern-day St. Augustine. He named the region for its wealth of flowers—*Florida* in Spanish. He did not find the fountain, but he found a strong northward current— the Gulf Stream—that would speed up sea travel to Europe.

France wanted a share of the riches from the Americas. Some people also wanted to leave France for religious reasons. They briefly established a colony called Charlesfort in South Carolina in 1562. When Charlesfort failed, they established a second colony, Fort Caroline, in Florida, about 35 miles (55 km) north of St. Augustine.

▲ René de Laudonnière led a second French expedition, which set up Fort Caroline at the mouth of the St. Johns River in Florida.

From Fort to Town

Although Juan Ponce de León landed in St. Augustine, he did not name it. That honor fell to Pedro Menéndez de Avilés. He founded the colony in 1565, naming it after a Catholic saint who lived hundreds of years earlier. For 20 years, Spanish settlers lived peacefully with the local American Indians, and St. Augustine grew in size and prospered.

▶ Spain's king named St. Augustine a *presidio*— a city that is an official military fortress of the Spanish Empire. It is the oldest continuous settlement in the United States.

▶ A cutaway of an explorer's ship. Supplies, such as beer, wine, and barrels of drinking water, were stored in the hold. Eating and sleeping areas were below the main deck, and the captain's cabin was at the stern, or rear.

The French are beaten

In 1565, France sent 600 soldiers and settlers to Fort Caroline. The Spanish king decided that French expansion must stop. He sent Admiral Pedro Menéndez to St. Augustine to do the job. The French leader tried to attack St. Augustine, but a hurricane blew his ships too far south. Meanwhile, Menéndez attacked Fort Caroline, killing most of the settlers. He then marched south and killed the French soldiers who had been shipwrecked. This ended French challenges to Spanish claims in North America.

▼ A Spanish rapier of the 1500s with a steel blade and a fancy cage hilt

◀ This sturdy, 90-foot (27-m)-long caravel is typical of the ships that explorers sailed across the Atlantic Ocean.

A Ship's Sorry Menu

Much of the food taken on voyages —such as crackers, oatmeal, flour, and peas—was dried. Ships also carried beef, pork, and cod, all salted to prevent spoilage. Still, over a period of months, spoilage did occur, and sailors were forced to eat partially rotted food to survive. Butter, salt, and vinegar rounded out the menu.

▶ The French explorer Jean Ribault met with Chief Athore of the Timucua Indians at Fort Caroline.

Drake's Lust for Gold
Europe fights over America's riches

By the late 1500s, a new enemy, England, threatened Spain's dominance in the Americas. Experienced English sailors, called sea dogs, thought it great sport to attack Spanish ships laden with treasure.

One of the most famous sea dogs was Francis Drake. He was raised by the Hawkins family, who were his relatives as well as merchants and pirates. Drake joined the family fleet and soon commanded his own ship in the Caribbean. On one expedition, he crossed the Isthmus of Panama—the strip of land joining North and South America that separates the Atlantic and Pacific oceans. On seeing the Pacific Ocean, he prayed to sail an English ship there one day.

Along the western coast of America

A few years later, Drake's wish came true. Queen Elizabeth I of England chose Drake to lead an expedition around the southern tip of South America. His secret mission was to plunder Spanish wealth. He set sail in December 1577. By September 1578, he had sailed into the Pacific Ocean and up the coasts of South and North America, anchoring briefly in San Francisco Bay. Then he sailed west across the Pacific and around the southern tip of Africa, arriving in England almost three years after he had left.

▲ Looted Spanish coins—doubloons and reales

◄ Drake landed near San Francisco in 1580 and named the land New Albion.

Picking Spanish Pockets
The Spanish treated the Pacific Ocean as their own private lake, not protecting their ships. When Drake sailed along South America, he had a heyday taking gold and silver off ships. One crew member recalled, "We found by the seaside a Spaniard lying asleep who had lying beside him 13 bars of silver which weighed 4,000 ducats Spanish. We took the silver and left the man."

Drake brings wealth back to his queen

Along the Pacific coast, Drake and his men boarded a series of Spanish ships, stripping each of its wealth. By far the biggest prize was the ship *Cacafuego*. On it they found pearls, precious stones, much gold, and tons of silver. When Drake reached the Molucca Islands in Southeast Asia, he added valuable spices to his cargo.

He reached Plymouth harbor in England in September 1580. As he landed, his first question was whether the queen was alive and well. Most of the treasure he brought back went to the queen's coffers. Queen Elizabeth boarded his famous ship, the *Golden Hind*, where she rewarded him with a title of nobility. She also gave Sir Francis Drake a large sum of money for this bold voyage. Drake was a hero, both to his queen and to the English people. But the Spanish called him *El Draque*, meaning "The Dragon."

▲ This seaman's compass, in an ivory case, was made around 1570. The continued exploration of the American coast led to increased knowledge about the continent.

Raid on St. Augustine

In 1585, Queen Elizabeth put Sir Francis Drake in charge of a fleet of 25 ships. His mission was to cause damage to Spain's overseas holdings. In addition to a series of other cities, Drake attacked St. Augustine in 1586 and ordered his men to burn the city. The colored engraving of Drake's taking of St. Augustine below is the earliest known engraved image of a U.S. city.

▼ England's Queen Elizabeth I, adorned with jewels

▼ *El Draque* attacks a Spanish treasure ship.

Queen Elizabeth's Heroes

In 1588, Spain gathered a huge fleet of ships, called the Spanish Armada, to attack England. Spain wanted to weaken England's power in Europe and stop the queen's sponsoring of pirates. Bad weather and an English fleet led by Drake and John Hawkins defeated the Armada. This marked the end of Spain's control of the world's sea lanes.

13

Raleigh and Roanoke
English colonies lost and found

As Spain's power in North America declined, England's rose. It attempted to set up colonies. One of these, Roanoke, came to a mysterious end. But in 1607, the first permanent English settlement was founded.

Queen Elizabeth granted another sea dog, Sir Walter Raleigh, the right to explore and settle the land around the Chesapeake Bay of North America. Raleigh named this land Virginia in honor of Elizabeth, who, being unmarried, was called the Virgin Queen. He wrote of America, "I shall yet live to see it an Inglishe nation."

In 1585, Raleigh sponsored an expedition that landed on Roanoke Island. The settlement failed because of conflicts with local American Indians. Another group settled Roanoke in 1587. This group of 150 people included 17 women and 9 children. Virginia Dare was born shortly after the colonists arrived—the first English person to be born in North America. Governor John White returned to England for supplies. Because of England's conflict with Spain, White could not go back for three years. By then, the settlement had disappeared.

▶ Sir Walter Raleigh was a favorite courtier of Queen Elizabeth I.

▼ Colonists used small rowboats to bring goods ashore.

The Lost Colony
When White returned to Roanoke in 1590, all he found were abandoned dwellings and the word CROATOAN carved on a post. White planned to go to Croatoan Island to see if the settlers were there, but a storm kept his ship from landing. Roanoke became known as the Lost Colony.

The founding of Jamestown

In 1607, a group of 105 colonists established a colony on the James River. It was 60 miles (96 km) north of Roanoke. They named it Jamestown, after James I, who became England's ruler when Elizabeth died. The colony had difficulty surviving. Many colonists did not want to work. Captain John Smith became the president of Jamestown in 1608. He made a new rule: "He that will not work shall not eat . . ." Thanks to Smith, Jamestown thrived and became a permanent settlement.

◄ John White painted this watercolor of an American Indian in about 1585.

▼ Settlers and American Indians often battled over land rights.

Tobacco

Tobacco was the crop that saved Jamestown. It became extremely popular in England. This leather pouch (left) may have belonged to Sir Walter Raleigh. It contains two clay pipes with silver mountings and a bone tobacco stopper. When Raleigh's servant first saw his master smoking, he thought he was on fire and threw water on him.

Success and growth

The local American Indians often helped the settlers, but they also attacked without warning. The settlers wanted to be independent of the American Indians yet learn their customs.

Many American Indians smoked tobacco. Sir Walter Raleigh tried it, enjoyed it, and introduced it to the English. Its popularity skyrocketed. One Jamestown colonist, John Rolfe, developed a way of curing tobacco in order for it to be exported. In 1614, Jamestown shipped its first tobacco crop to England.

Other colonists imitated Rolfe's methods. By 1620, Jamestown was a thriving colony.

15

Opening Up the Interior
Exploration inland along the waterways

Through the 1600s, explorers from France, England, Spain, Italy, and the Netherlands tried to find a way west through the continent of North America to China. All failed. Meanwhile, English and French explorers continued to claim American land for their countries.

Just two years after Pizarro seized the fabulous wealth of the Incas, France began exploration of the northern part of North America. Jacques Cartier sailed up the St. Lawrence River in 1535. He and his men spent a terrible winter near present-day Quebec. The hardships they suffered—bitter cold, disease, and fear of attack from American Indians—persuaded French rulers not to pursue further exploration inland for more than 70 years.

▶ This map of North and Central America from the early 1700s shows that by then only the eastern half of the continent had been surveyed.

▲▼ Frenchman La Salle canoed down the Mississippi River, reaching its mouth on April 9, 1682.

Reestablishing a Presence
In 1672, the governor of New France—the name for French territory in North America—asked explorer Louis Jolliet and missionary Jacques Marquette to explore the Mississippi River. Ten years later, René-Robert Cavelier, Sieur de La Salle, sailed down the Mississippi River to the Gulf of Mexico. New contacts were made with American Indians.

▶ Englishman Henry Hudson and his son, adrift among the ice floes of Hudson Bay

Hudson Travels North
Henry Hudson explored New York for the Dutch in 1609. The following year, he sailed farther north for England, searching for a passage to the Pacific Ocean. He spent the winter on Hudson Bay, in Canada's frozen north. His men refused to continue the next spring. They forced him, his son, and five sailors into a small boat. Hudson was never heard from again.

Success with trade and territory

The American Indians told the French of huge rivers and lakes farther west. This prompted the French to continue to look for a waterway route to the Pacific Ocean. However, by 1673, La Salle had traveled far enough on the Mississippi to know that it did not empty into the Pacific. On the journey he helped set up a profitable fur trade with the American Indians. He also proclaimed the land of the Mississippi River basin "Louisiana," after the French king, Louis XIV. In 1687, La Salle set up a small colony in what is now Texas.

◀ **Marquette and Jolliet explored the Mississippi River from its source in present-day Minnesota.**

Jolliet and Marquette Travel South

Jacques Marquette spoke five American Indian languages and knew the ways of American Indian peoples who lived around the Great Lakes. Marquette and Jolliet were the first white men to travel the Mississippi from its source in Minnesota to where it is joined by the Arkansas River.

Spreading the word

The combination of missionary and explorer was not uncommon in New France. In the 1600s, missionaries came to New France in greater numbers to convert American Indians to Catholicism. To do so, they needed to learn the American Indians' languages and ways. American Indians called the missionaries Black Robes, after the clothing they wore.

The Jesuit missionaries made reports back to their churches in France. They discussed the beliefs and lifestyles of American Indians as well as the climate and resources of the land. Often, it was the missionaries who informed Europeans about the New World.

Samuel de Champlain

In 1608, French explorer Samuel de Champlain founded the settlement of Quebec. He brought settlers with him, but the colony grew slowly. In this picture from the time, Champlain is attacking an American Indian fort in present-day western New York State.

Spanish Missions
Southern and western Spanish America

Like France, Spain sent missionaries to North America to convert American Indians. But the Spanish did not begin this activity until the late 1600s. They continued through the early 1800s.

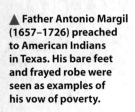

The Spanish government in North and Central America was called New Spain. New Spain was concerned about the lack of settlements in its northern reaches—what are today Texas and California. The government invited Spanish monks to come to North America to establish missions. The missions were set up to convert native people to Catholicism and to colonize the areas, strengthening the Spanish presence in America. This was of utmost importance, as English, Russian, French, and even American explorers and traders trespassed on Spanish lands.

▲ **Father Antonio Margil (1657–1726) preached to American Indians in Texas. His bare feet and frayed robe were seen as examples of his vow of poverty.**

Founding Fathers

Two Franciscan monks carved places in American history with their founding of missions. In Texas, Father Antonio Margil founded two missions and was the leader of those and four additional missions. Father Margil is credited with the beginning of European Texas. In California, Father Junípero Serra founded nine missions from San Diego to Sonoma, a distance of about 700 miles (1,130 km). He is considered the "father of California."

Like a Small Town

This picture shows daily life at Mission San Carlos Borromeo, located in Carmel, California. It was the second California mission, founded by Father Serra in 1771. The mission converts grew grains and vegetables and raised horses and cattle. It had two *rancheras*—places where the horses were stabled. By 1795, 875 converts lived at the mission. This was Father Serra's home mission, and he is buried under the sanctuary floor.

Mission life

The fathers came with soldiers, priests, and builders. As soon as they had set up a mission, they encouraged local American Indians to come and stay. The fathers offered three meals a day and protection from more aggressive neighbors. Once there, however, the converts had to work for no pay and could not leave without permission. This caused some of them to liken their condition to slavery.

Life on a mission was hard. American Indians were not used to living on a strict schedule. Everyone rose early for Mass, prayers, and breakfast. They had jobs to do as well as religious instruction. They went to bed early. They missed their villages and families. Some converts ran away but were caught and brought back.

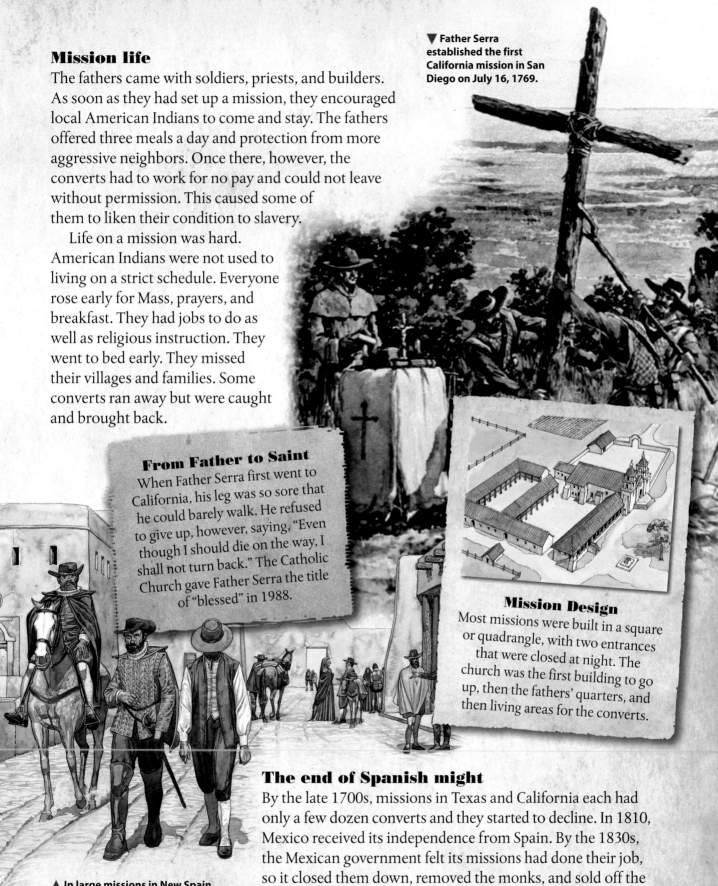

▼ Father Serra established the first California mission in San Diego on July 16, 1769.

From Father to Saint

When Father Serra first went to California, his leg was so sore that he could barely walk. He refused to give up, however, saying, "Even though I should die on the way, I shall not turn back." The Catholic Church gave Father Serra the title of "blessed" in 1988.

Mission Design

Most missions were built in a square or quadrangle, with two entrances that were closed at night. The church was the first building to go up, then the fathers' quarters, and then living areas for the converts.

▲ In large missions in New Spain, American Indians and Spanish settlers lived in separate areas.

The end of Spanish might

By the late 1700s, missions in Texas and California each had only a few dozen converts and they started to decline. In 1810, Mexico received its independence from Spain. By the 1830s, the Mexican government felt its missions had done their job, so it closed them down, removed the monks, and sold off the land. Today, most of the missions are historic sites.

Lewis and Clark

An expedition to western North America

By 1800, English, Russian, and American ships were sailing along the Pacific coast, trading with American Indians. In 1803, 27 years after the birth of the United States, the president set up a search for a waterway linking the Atlantic and Pacific oceans.

▲ In 1792, Captain Robert Gray explored and named the Columbia River, which gave the United States a claim to Oregon Territory.

▼ British Captain James Cook explored the waters around Alaska in 1779. Here, his ships are anchored in Prince William Sound.

President Thomas Jefferson asked Meriwether Lewis, his private secretary, to form the Corps of Discovery to make the expedition. Lewis's knowledge of plants and animals would be of great value. Lewis chose William Clark as his coleader. He and Clark had served together in the army on the Ohio frontier and were comfortable in the wild.

While the expedition was forming, the United States purchased the Louisiana Territory from France. Stretching from the Mississippi River to the Rocky Mountains, this land doubled the size of the nation. Now, more than ever, there was good reason to explore the country.

▶ This compass in a wooden case is like the one used by Lewis and Clark.

▼ Lewis and Clark were joined by Clark's slave, York; Lewis's dog, Scannon; and a Shoshone guide, Sacagawea, and her baby.

Daniel Boone

The land between settled areas in the East and the wilderness in the West was known as the frontier, and the men who explored it were called frontiersmen. One such man was Daniel Boone. Boone explored Kentucky several times in the 1760s and 1770s. In 1775, the Transylvania Company hired him to blaze a trail through the Cumberland Gap in the Appalachian Mountains. The group set a route for the Wilderness Road, which became the main route to Kentucky from the East and opened the way for settlers heading to Texas and beyond.

▲ Daniel Boone leading settlers through the Cumberland Gap

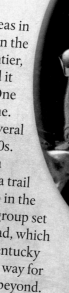

necessary to carry into effect ...

expedition. ————

Part of the estimate of costs that Meriwether Lewis wrote up before the Corps of Discovery set out

...thematical Instruments &. 217. ~

...arms Accoutrements extraordinary " . 81. ~

Camp Equipage . " . 255. ~

Medicine & packing . 55. ~

...transportation 30. ~

Instructions from the President

President Jefferson instructed Lewis to take the Corps of Discovery expedition up the Missouri River and follow it to its source. Then he was to cross the Rocky Mountains and travel down the newly discovered Columbia River to the Pacific. The president also wanted him to gather information on the plants, animals, soil, climate, and minerals of the land. Equally important was meeting the American Indians along the way, making friends if possible, and exploring the chances for future trade with them.

... 00.

" . 87.

Total $. 2,500.

Mapping and exploring new territory

Lewis and Clark worked through the winter of 1803–1804 to prepare for the journey. Both leaders believed in firm discipline and ran the expedition as if it were a small army. There were also times of fun and celebration, however. The corps of 45 men and one dog left St. Charles, Missouri, on May 21, 1804. Going upstream on the Missouri River, they traveled about 15 miles (24 km) a day. By August, they were in present-day Nebraska. The Great Plains stretched out before them.

The corps began to see animals that probably no white person had ever seen before: pronghorn antelope, prairie dogs, coyotes, and horned toads. Lewis was overwhelmed by the "immense herds of Buffalo, deer Elk and Antelopes …"

Reaching the Pacific
Traveling by water, horse, and foot

"Ocean in view! O! the joy!" wrote Clark on November 7, 1805, as the expedition paddled down the mighty Columbia River. It had crossed the Great Plains and struggled over the Rocky Mountains, helped by American Indians.

By the winter of 1804, Lewis and Clark built Fort Mandan in present-day North Dakota, where they rested until April. As they left winter camp, Lewis noted, "We were about to penetrate a country at least two thousand miles in width, on which the foot of civilized man had never before trodden . . ."

Traveling along rivers and over mountains was backbreaking work. They often had to tow their boats, and several people almost drowned. When they reached the Pacific, they were cold, hungry, and exhausted.

▶ Lewis and Clark used canoes to navigate the wild waters of the Columbia and other western rivers. Sometimes the men had to carry the boats around obstacles.

▶ William Clark's journal of the trip. The journal is now kept at the Missouri Historical Society in St. Louis, Missouri.

Recording All They Saw

An essential purpose of the expedition was to record what they saw, for both the president and the country as a whole. Clark was an expert at drawing maps, and he used this ability to map out the territory that they covered each day. Both men kept journals of the expedition. Lewis also gathered specimens of soil, plants, and sometimes animals to be sent back to President Jefferson.

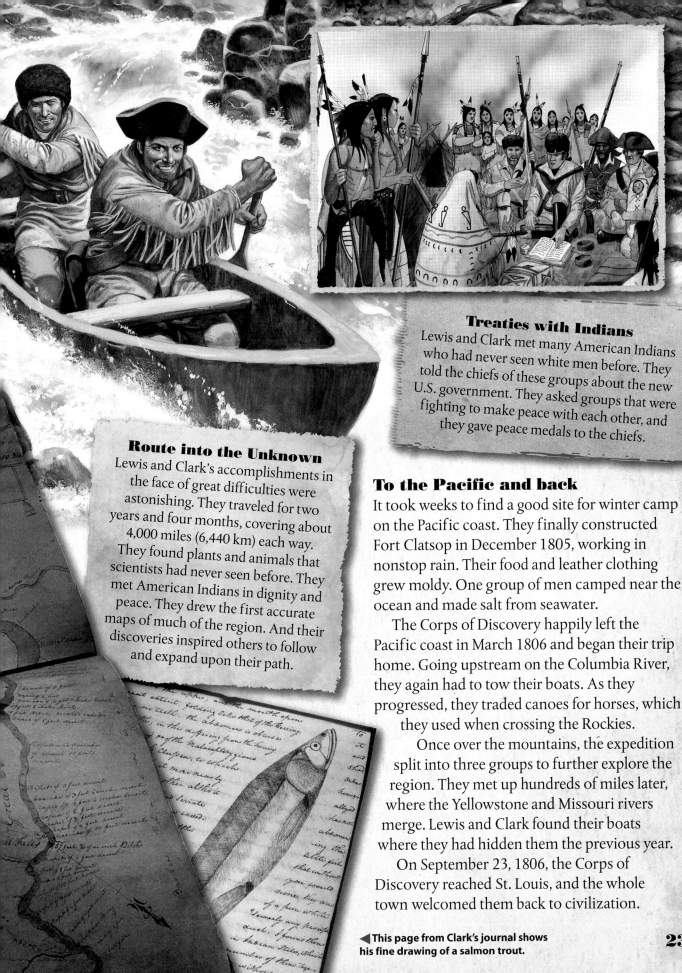

Treaties with Indians

Lewis and Clark met many American Indians who had never seen white men before. They told the chiefs of these groups about the new U.S. government. They asked groups that were fighting to make peace with each other, and they gave peace medals to the chiefs.

Route into the Unknown

Lewis and Clark's accomplishments in the face of great difficulties were astonishing. They traveled for two years and four months, covering about 4,000 miles (6,440 km) each way. They found plants and animals that scientists had never seen before. They met American Indians in dignity and peace. They drew the first accurate maps of much of the region. And their discoveries inspired others to follow and expand upon their path.

To the Pacific and back

It took weeks to find a good site for winter camp on the Pacific coast. They finally constructed Fort Clatsop in December 1805, working in nonstop rain. Their food and leather clothing grew moldy. One group of men camped near the ocean and made salt from seawater.

The Corps of Discovery happily left the Pacific coast in March 1806 and began their trip home. Going upstream on the Columbia River, they again had to tow their boats. As they progressed, they traded canoes for horses, which they used when crossing the Rockies.

Once over the mountains, the expedition split into three groups to further explore the region. They met up hundreds of miles later, where the Yellowstone and Missouri rivers merge. Lewis and Clark found their boats where they had hidden them the previous year.

On September 23, 1806, the Corps of Discovery reached St. Louis, and the whole town welcomed them back to civilization.

◀ **This page from Clark's journal shows his fine drawing of a salmon trout.**

Trade and Treaties

Pushing the frontier westward

During Lewis and Clark's trip, one man, John Colter, left the expedition and remained in the West to trap animals for their fur. Colter and other frontiersmen further opened up the United States.

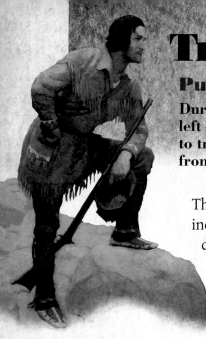

The fur trade grew as Europeans' demand for furs increased. Gentlemen wore beaver hats, and ladies wore dresses and bonnets trimmed with fur. The supply of beaver pelts in the eastern Rocky Mountains seemed endless. Mountain men supplied the furs. Mountain men lived in the Rockies and trapped most of the year. Living in the wild, their skin grew as dark as American Indians'. They had beards, wore their hair long, and dressed in buckskin. Once a year, they met at a rendezvous and traded furs for money and supplies. The meeting became a time of celebration—with games, conversation, and drinking—that frontiersmen looked forward to all year.

▲ Dressed in buckskins, mountain men owned little more than their clothes, a rifle, knives, beaver traps, and a horse.

▲ James Beckwourth was an African-American slave whose owner freed him. He became a mountain man, fur trader, and explorer in the West.

A Life of High Adventure

Frontiersmen found great places that no white man had seen before, such as Yellowstone and Yosemite, which are now national parks. They fought grizzly bears and other animals and lived to tell the tale. In fact, their tales were often hard to believe. Mountain man Jim Bridger noted, "They said I was the [darnedest] liar ever lived. That's what a man gets for telling the truth."

▲ Mountain men traded with American Indians. They offered blankets, knives, and kettles in exchange for beaver furs. They then sold the furs to trading companies.

▼ As settlers moved west, the U.S. government forced American Indians from their homelands onto reservations, changing their lives forever.

Buying Up Much of the West

Between 1803 and 1853, the United States tripled in size. In 1803, the purchase of the Louisiana Territory for $15 million extended the country's borders to the Rockies. In 1845, Texas became a state, and in 1846, Oregon Territory became part of the nation. After the Mexican-American War of 1846–1848, Mexico sold to the United States land stretching from Wyoming and Colorado to California, followed by parts of Arizona and New Mexico. The borders of the nation were now complete.

▲ In 1846, Mexico and the United States fought over land in the Southwest.

Treaties with American Indians

Since mountain men were not employed by the government, they could not form treaties with American Indians. However, Major Stephen H. Long, who explored the Platte River for the U.S. Army Corps of Engineers, could. In 1820, Long met with the Pawnee, Oto, and Omaha Indians and made treaties with them. Long also described the Great Plains as the "Great Desert," which for many years deterred settlers from setting up homes there.

Opening up the continent

The frontiersmen explored the West and informed others of its wonders and perils. John Colter was the first white man to see the geysers and bubbling mud of today's Yellowstone. Tom Fitzpatrick explored South Pass, a notch in the Rocky Mountains through which thousands of settlers later poured. Jedediah Smith and Joe Walker explored routes to the California coast.

By 1840, Europeans were no longer interested in beaver fur for top hats. Moreover, the beaver population had drastically declined. The year 1840 marked the last rendezvous, and mountain men looked elsewhere for work.

The Great Surveys
Paving the way for land rushes

After the Civil War of 1861–1865, the U.S. government organized a series of surveys of the West. They were called the Great Surveys. They crisscrossed the region, adding depth to Americans' appreciation of their great land.

Four men headed up the Great Surveys, which recorded details of the landscape and natural features of the country. Clarence King led the first of the surveys, beginning in 1867. His Fortieth Parallel Survey examined a 100-mile (160-km) band of land that stretched from the Sierra Nevada in California to the Nebraska border. In 1869, John Wesley Powell surveyed the canyon lands in the Southwest. Then Congress granted him funds to travel down the Colorado River through the Grand Canyon.

▲ A surveyor is photographed with the tools of his trade—a transit on a tripod and dividers. A transit is used in mapmaking to measure angles on the ground.

This 1846 map shows Oregon and Upper (or "New") California.

Deeds and Quests

Surveying lands led to great discoveries and adventures. Clarence King was once hit by lightning and survived. Ferdinand Hayden found the Yellowstone wonders that John Colter had told about decades earlier. Hayden persuaded the government to name it the first national park in 1872. John Wesley Powell had great respect for the American Indians he met. In 1879, he persuaded Congress to establish the Bureau of Ethnology, which studied American Indian cultures.

Charting the coast and mountains

Also in 1869, Lieutenant George Wheeler began a survey that extended from Oregon to the Mexican border and from eastern Colorado to the Sierra Nevada. In the final survey of 1878, Ferdinand Hayden mapped the Rocky Mountain region.

▼ In this 1883 photograph, members of the United States Geological Survey measure a map line near Fort Wingate, New Mexico.

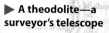
► A theodolite—a surveyor's telescope

▲ Members of the British North American Boundary Commission rest during the marking of the boundary separating the United States from Canada.

Turning Resources into Homes

Wherever they ended up, settlers used the available resources to construct homes and other buildings. Where there were forests, settlers cut down trees and used the wood for building. On the Great Plains, settlers cut blocks of soil from the earth and built sod houses. Settlers in the Southwest used adobe bricks of clay and straw for construction.

▲ Settlers eagerly moved to the new lands. They followed routes described by the surveyors, crossing the rivers and plains by flatboat, wagon, horse, and foot.

▶ John Wesley Powell made two trips down the Colorado River, proving his idea that the river cut out the canyons as the land rose over millions of years.

Following the trails out West

Pioneers—people who looked for ideal places for settlements—were right on the heels of the frontiersmen and surveyors, often using the surveys to find their way. Frontiersmen and surveyors also guided settlers coming across the overland trails in wagon trains.

Early settlers who moved to the West were usually farmers looking for good farmland or miners looking for gold or silver. Beginning in the 1840s, they followed the Oregon Trail or the California Trail.

Population spread and growth

White people began to fill lands that only American Indians had lived on. Once the transcontinental railroad was completed in 1869, people began to move out West by train rather than wagon train. First the West Coast became populated, then the Great Plains. By 1870, the number of people living in the United States had reached almost 40 million— an increase of 16 million in just 20 years.

Spanning the Continent
Maps are completed and the nation settled

Even before the Great Surveys, railroad companies hired surveyors to make maps of unknown lands across the continent. Then the government encouraged settlers to move to these lands and to the last remaining unclaimed territory.

▲ An early railroad surveyor

Government officials understood the benefits of a country connected by rail. Goods and people could be transported by railroad more easily, quickly, and safely than by river or road. Also, the Civil War had shown that railroads allowed for easy transportation of troops. Railroads aided the postal service, which had previously been slow and unreliable, and allowed Americans access to the wonders of the West. Railroads made settlement of the West easier than it had ever been before. The national government helped the railroad companies build railroads in another way: it granted millions of acres of public land to the railroads, on either side of the actual tracks. The companies paid for the construction of the railroads by selling this land to settlers.

▼ Railroad surveyors pose with their transits on tripods, their measuring rods, and their dog.

► This poster advertised a rail route to government land to be given over to farms.

Railroads Sell Off Land

Railroad offices advertised the sale of their land, printing handbills that were spread by sea travelers beyond the continent to northern Europe. In the 1870s, for example, people from Germany came to Nebraska and Kansas and formed more than 40 percent of the population of some towns. The population of Minnesota nearly doubled between 1880 and 1890 because of the influx of Scandinavians.

2,000,00
CENTRA
30 Milli
YOU NE
NORT
HOW T

Not Everyone's a Winner

Since the 1830s, present-day Oklahoma had been known as Indian Territory, set aside for American Indian tribes that had been forced there from farther east. Although the U.S. government had promised the land to the American Indians forever, it broke its treaties. Because the Indians supported the Confederacy during the Civil War, they were punished by having much of their land in Indian Territory taken away.

Mixed fortunes

Settling on the plains was a risky operation, even if the land was free or dirt-cheap. Homesteaders built houses from sod, and some walked miles just to get water. To homesteader Howard Ruede, Kansas was heaven on earth. He was proud of the potatoes he grew "that weighed over a pound [450 g] a piece . . ." To others, the prairie was more like hell than heaven.

The last great land rush

The last land to be opened up for settlement was Oklahoma Territory. The Oklahoma Land Rush took place on April 22, 1889. On that day the government opened 1.9 million acres (770,000 ha) for settlement. For weeks before, thousands of settlers had been lining up at the territory borders. When the bugler blew his horn at noon, the land rush began. Towns literally sprang up overnight. By 1890, the United States was a truly settled land with a population of nearly 63 million.

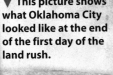

◀ In this land office in Kansas in 1874, settlers choose homesteads from a map of the available land.

People in wagons and on horseback raced to stake their claims.

▼ This picture shows what Oklahoma City looked like at the end of the first day of the land rush.

Guthrie, an Overnight Town

A reporter wrote about the town of Guthrie, Oklahoma: "Unlike Rome, the city of Guthrie was built in a day . . . It might be said that it was built in an afternoon. At twelve o'clock on Monday, April 22 [1889], the resident population of Guthrie was nothing; before sundown it was at least ten thousand."

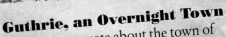

Glossary

adobe bricks that are dried in the sun

archaeologist a person who studies past cultures and ancient settlements

California Trail the overland trail leading to California that settlers followed in the mid-1800s

colony a settlement ruled by a faraway country

conquistador a Spanish conqueror

expedition a journey made for a purpose, such as exploring the land

frontier the edge of a settled area

homestead land given to a settler by the U.S. government

Louisiana Purchase the huge tract of land west of the Mississippi River purchased from France in 1803

mission the living and working quarters of missionaries

missionary a person who tries to convert others to his or her religion

mountain men traders and fur trappers who lived in the Rocky Mountains from the 1820s to the 1840s

Oregon Trail the overland trail leading to the Willamette Valley in Oregon that settlers followed in the mid-1800s

pioneer a person who does something first for others, such as settlers, to follow

pirate an outlaw sea commander whose ship attacked, raided, and looted treasure from other ships or from harbors

plains a wide area of flat or gently rolling land. The Great Plains is land between the Mississippi River and the Rockies

plant the term used by the English for establishing a settlement that would eventually become a colony

prairie a large area of grassy land with few or no trees

rendezvous the yearly gatherings of mountain men to exchange furs for money and to socialize. The word comes from two French words meaning "present yourselves."

reservation an area of land set aside by the U.S. government for American Indians to live on

Rocky Mountains the main mountain system in the western United States; also known as the Rockies

Scandinavia a region of northern Europe including Sweden, Norway, Denmark, and sometimes Iceland and Finland

sea dog an experienced sailor and often pirate of an English sailing warship

settlement any place where people live

settler someone new who comes to an area and sets up home

sod the top layer of earth, held together by matted grass roots and used as a building material on the plains

South Pass a valley in the Rocky Mountains that was a gateway to the West on the Oregon Trail

survey the act of deciding the boundaries and shape of land by measuring; also to inspect, examine, or map land

territory land owned and governed by the United States but is not yet a state

transcontinental railroad the railroad that connected the eastern and western parts of the United States

treaty an agreement to maintain peace

wagon train a group of wagons traveling west together. A long line of wagons looked like the cars of a train.

Timeline

about 1000 Vikings establish the settlement of Vinland in Newfoundland

1492 Christopher Columbus reaches islands in the Caribbean Sea

1497 John Cabot explores the eastern coast of Canada

1502 Amerigo Vespucci explores the South American coastline for Spain

1513 Vasco Núñez de Balboa is the first European to see the Pacific Ocean from the Americas

1513 Juan Ponce de León explores the Florida coast

1535 Jacques Cartier sails up the St. Lawrence River

1562 France tries to establish Charlesfort colony

1565 St. Augustine, the oldest permanent settlement in the United States, is founded in Florida

1585; 1587 A colony at Roanoke is established

1590 Roanoke colony found to have disappeared

1607 Jamestown becomes the first permanent English settlement in North America

1608 Samuel de Champlain founds Quebec for France

1609 Henry Hudson explores New York

1673 Jacques Marquette and Louis Jolliet explore the Mississippi River for France

1682 René-Robert Cavelier, Sieur de La Salle, claims the entire Mississippi River basin for France

1769 First Spanish mission in California is established

1775 Daniel Boone blazes the Wilderness Road

1776 Declaration of Independence: birth of the U.S.A.

1803 The Louisiana Purchase is completed

1804–1806 The Lewis and Clark Expedition

1841 The first organized wagon trains head west

1845 Texas becomes a state

1846 The United States and Great Britain set the present boundary between the United States and Canada

1846 Oregon Territory becomes part of the nation

1848 The United States pays $15 million to Mexico for California and areas of the Southwest

1853 In the Gadsden Purchase, the United States buys southern New Mexico and Arizona from Mexico

1862 Homestead Act is passed

1867–1878 The Great Surveys of the West take place

1869 Transcontinental railroad is completed

1889 Oklahoma Land Rush

Information

WEBSITES

The Vikings—National Museum of Natural History
www.mnh.si.edu/vikings/

Conquistadors
www.pbs.org/conquistadors/

California Missions
http://californias-missions.org/index.html

Lewis and Clark
www.pbs.org/lewisandclark/

Frontiersmen—Museum of the Mountain Man
www.museumofthemountainman.com/

United States Geological Survey
www.usgs.gov/aboutusgs/who_we_are/ history.asp

History of Railroads and Maps—Library of Congress
http://memory.loc.gov/ammem/gmdhtml/ rrhtml/rrintro.html

BOOKS TO READ

Berger, Melvin, and Gilda Berger. *The Real Vikings: Craftsmen, Traders, and Fearsome Raiders*. Washington, DC: National Geographic, 2003.

Fradin, Dennis Brindell, and Judith Bloom Fradin. *Who Was Sacagawea?* New York: Grosset & Dunlap, 2002.

Isaacs, Sally Senzell. *The Lewis and Clark Expedition*. Chicago, IL: Heinemann Library, 2004.

Manheimer, Ann S. *James Beckwourth: Legendary Mountain Man*. Minneapolis, MN: Twenty-First Century Books, 2006.

Nick, Charles. *Sir Francis Drake: Slave Trader and Pirate*. New York: Franklin Watts, 2009.

Wade, Mary Dodson. *Christopher Columbus*. New York: Children's Press, 2003.

West, David, Jackie Gaff, and Jim Eldridge. *Hernán Cortés: The Life of a Spanish Conquistador*. New York: Rosen Publishing, 2005.

Index